Helping your pupils
to think for themselves

The Little Books of Life Skills

In our rapidly changing world, education is becoming less and less about imparting knowledge than it is about empowerment. We now want to make sure our children get the skills they need, not only to engage with and take responsibility for their own learning, but to successfully take part in a range of experiences throughout their lives.

The strategies and activities in the *Little Books of Life Skills* will help children see themselves as champions of their own world, a critical step in meeting the outcomes of the **Every Child Matters** agenda. Each title in the series will help children get the skills they need to enjoy and achieve – in school and beyond.

The five *Little Books of Life Skills* are:

- *Helping your pupils to ask questions*
- *Helping your pupils to be resilient*
- *Helping your pupils to communicate effectively and manage conflict*
- *Helping your pupils to think for themselves*
- *Helping your pupils to work cooperatively*

Helping your pupils
to think for themselves

Jeni Wilson and Kath Murdoch

Routledge
Taylor & Francis Group

LONDON AND NEW YORK

First published by Curriculum Corporation 2006
PO Box 177
Carlton South Vic 3053
Australia

This edition published 2008 by Routledge
2 Park Square, Milton Park, Abingdon, Oxon, OX14 4RN, United Kingdom

Simultaneously published in the USA and Canada
by Routledge
711 Third Ave, New York, NY 10017

Routledge is an imprint of the Taylor & Francis Group, an informa business

© 2006, 2008 Jeni Wilson and Kath Murdoch

Illustrations by Aja Bongiorno
Typeset in Stone Serif by FiSH Books, Enfield, Middx.

Dedication
To Ethan, Madison, Gretta and Holly. We hope they continue to challenge their own – and our – thinking.

Acknowledgements
Many of the examples in this book have been trialled in classrooms. For their willingness to share their ideas we acknowledge the contributions of and thank: Kim Wise, Brunswick South East PS; Vanessa Forster and Joy Moodley, St Albans East PS; Kathryn Palmer, Michele Di Camillo and Robyn Smith, Killara PS; Marc Browne and Jodie Mantach, Grovedale PS; Michael McGough, Melanie Treweek and the Grade 5/6 team, Apollo Parkways PS; Moira Turner, Skipton PS; teachers and pupils from Hawthorn West PS, Princes Hill PS and Roberts McCubbin PS.

The table on pages 14–15 was adapted from Wilson & Wing Jan (2003); the concepts on page 40 were adapted from Murdoch & Hornsby (1998).

British Library Cataloguing in Publication Data
A catalogue record for this book is available from the British Library

Library of Congress Cataloging in Publication Data
A catalog record has been requested for this book

ISBN 10: 0-415-44730-5
ISBN 13: 978-0-415-44730-0

Contents

Contents

The importance of thinking

Thinking is central to learning. To this end, teachers have always been concerned with what, when and how their pupils think. Across the world, we are experiencing a shift to more pupil-centred approaches to learning – and this shift has brought about a new emphasis on the teaching of thinking. More and more educators are asking themselves: How can we help our pupils learn to be independent, creative, critical and reflective thinkers? How can we support pupils to think for themselves? Developing the capacity to think for themselves by using a variety of thinking skills is essential for pupils to become successful, lifelong learners who can successfully tackle a range of problems at school and beyond.

Planning for thinking in the classroom should be guided by a clear set of beliefs. The beliefs that underpin the strategies in this book are:

- Thinking is central to teaching and learning.
- Pupils think in different ways. A teaching program should acknowledge and accommodate these differences.
- Reflective thinking and metacognition enhance learning – and pupil ownership of learning.
- Thinking skills and questioning strategies can be taught. This is best done within the context of meaningful content and purposeful activities.
- Cooperative group work can enhance thinking. Dialogue, including a range of types of questioning (between pupils and between teachers and pupils), is vital to the development of thinking skills.
- Improving pupils' thinking takes time and a less cluttered curriculum.
- Developing pupils' thinking skills enhances learning across the curriculum and in a wide range of real-world learning situations.

If these beliefs are accepted, they offer a framework for developing a more thinking-oriented classroom.

Types of thinking

Before we can plan to teach thinking more effectively, we need to clarify our own understanding of what thinking actually is. To do this, it is helpful to establish the different kinds of thinking that we want our learners to do. There are many types of thinking and different types of thinking are required for different purposes. For example, if logical thinking doesn't solve a problem, creative thinking might be useful. Metacognition would also be used to help decide if new strategies are required.

While critical, creative and, to some extent, reflective thinking are often well understood and taught, metacognition – perhaps the most crucial type of thinking for pupil progress – is often misunderstood and, therefore, is less effectively translated into effective classroom practice. Metacognition involves active self-assessment, active decision making and personal goal setting. Involving pupils in their own thinking and learning in these ways is an important educational goal.

To be more specific, metacognition is when a learner (or teacher) is *aware* of their own thinking, *evaluates* their own thinking and *regulates* their own thinking. The following box provides examples of questions and statements that indicate metacognition.

Questions and statements indicating metacognition

> *What do I need to do here?* (Awareness)
> *I need to change my way of working.* (Regulation)
> *Am I making progress?* (Evaluation)
> *When I worry that I can't solve these problems, I never get them done.* (Awareness and evaluation)
> *The problem we did last week was similar to this...* (Awareness)
> *I am not good at these kinds of tasks.* (Evaluation)
> *My plan isn't working so I need to change the way I am approaching this task.* (Regulation)

Reflective thinking is also promoted as important for learning but it is not the same as metacognition. When we are being metacognitive, the focus of thinking is our own thinking, whereas reflective thinking is about something other than our own thinking.

Reflective thinking is deeper than just thinking about something – it refers to almost any purposeful thought where the learner engages in active, persistent and careful consideration of ideas for a deeper understanding. Dewey's (1933) conception is almost always referred to when attempting to define reflection. He described reflection as systematic and rigorous thinking used to resolve states of doubt, a question or a perplexity. Reflection and metacognition are keys to learning.

We learn from reflecting on experiences, feelings and beliefs. This is true for all learners (including teachers), therefore we need to strategically plan and teach for thinking in the context of authentic learner-centred classrooms, regardless of the age of the pupil or the subject area being taught.

Thinking can be organised in many ways but we have chosen three broad headings:

1 reflective thinking and metacognition

2 creative thinking

3 logical and critical thinking.

The thinking guide on pages 6–7 has been developed to assist teachers with planning to make the links between the thinking types and the associated skills, teacher questions and sample activities. The guide also gives examples of questions and comments which indicate that pupils are engaging in the type of thinking.

The lists in the thinking guide are not exhaustive, nor do they indicate that types of thinking should be discrete. Thinking usually involves skills in more than one category. In addition, skills such as synthesising could involve creative or critical thinking. For example, compare the difference between the synthesis of statistical and qualitative data. With these considerations in mind and to aid accessibility, the skills have been listed in one category only.

Similarly, the strategies have only been listed in one category to avoid repetition but many may be used in different ways and for different purposes. For example, de Bono's coloured thinking hats involve critical, creative and reflective thinking and metacognition, and many graphic organisers can be used for a range of purposes.

The thinking guide is not meant to be a sequential planner, nor is it intended that activities be contrived to cover all skills in any one lesson. By using the guide, a more balanced approach is possible. By the end of a sequence of learning events, most, if not all, types of thinking (but not necessarily all skills) would occur. The thinking audit below is designed to help teachers keep tabs on their coverage of thinking skills. Teachers are encouraged to add to the strategies and use it as a menu of ideas from which to select.

Thinking audit – example questions

Have you asked your pupils to:

- ask questions about their own thinking and learning and the world? (Reflective and metacognitive)
- make decisions about the learning process? (Reflective and metacognitive)
- consider how their ideas have changed? (Reflective and metacognitive)
- consider the impact on others? (Reflective and metacognitive)
- consider how others might feel or think about the issue? (Reflective and metacognitive)
- find and consider alternatives or solutions? (Creative)
- challenge assumptions? (Creative)
- imagine how things could be? (Creative)
- analyse data and information? (Critical)
- examine and critique data and information? (Critical)
- synthesise collected data or diverse data sets? (Critical)
- make judgements or evaluate ideas? (Critical)

See the extended list on page 63.

Thinking preferences

In addition to understanding the importance of thinking, we also now recognise that different learners have different thinking preferences – as distinct from skills. Generally, pupils who have a left-brain thinking preference feel more comfortable, capable and competent with thinking that involves reasoning and critiquing when they can examine, reason, organise, analyse,

At a glance thinking guide

I want my students to …

Think	So I ask …	I could try …	Pupils might say …
Reflection and metacognition			
self-question	How do you feel about …?	de Bono's shoes and hats	I wonder if …
question	How have you changed your thinking?	debate	I need to know …
make an action plan	As a result of what you've learnt, what do you plan to do?	question dice	I want to …
make decisions	How does this relate to your life?	brainstorm (list, describe, name)	How can I …?
apply the ideas to another situation	What would you like to find out?	role-play	I don't know how to …
recall	Why do you think …?	conscience game	I think I've done a problem like this before.
summarise	Tell me/show me what you already know about …	Graphic organisers:	Last time I did something like this I …
review and revise	What would other people feel/say about this?	• concept map	Next time I will …
think about others' feelings and perspectives	How might ____ be feeling?	• cluster web	I need to make a plan to work it out.
think ethically	What are other ways of looking at this?	• spider diagram	I remember when …
think empathically	How would this affect others?	• bridge	I know that …
		• comic strip	I've learnt …
		• CTG graph	I feel …
			They might feel/say …
			Another way of looking at this is …
Creative thinking			
create many original ideas	Can you construct/produce …?	forced relationship/ridiculous association	What if I changed …?
adapt ideas – add, expand, change	What's the most unusual …?	BAR (Bigger, Add, Remove)	I want to make something new.
find and consider alternatives and solutions	What if …?	the reverse key	If I added …
challenge assumptions	Suppose you …?	visualise	There must be other ways …
imagine	What would you never find/expect/see at …?	SCAMPER (Substitute, Combine, Adapt, Modify/ Magnify/Minimise,	I think … will happen if we …
	How many different ways could this problem be tackled?		There's lots of ways to …
			Why can't we try a new way?

predict	What are some different possibilities?	Put another way, Eliminate, Remove/Reverse	
hypothesise			
plan			
invent			

Logical and critical thinking

organise	How could you organise these ideas/objects?	bundling	I can put these types together …
classify	What are the important factors?	fat and skinny questions	The most important parts are …
analyse	If your findings are true for other … what can you now say about all …?	metaphors	I think that the … must …
examine		story maps	When you put all the ideas together it means …
critique	What would you expect might be the reason for or cause of …?	Graphic organisers:	You need to do it in this order …
generalise	How could you sum up the situation?	• cluster web	If you do … then … might happen.
hypothesise	Which would be more effective/ fairest? Where do you stand?	• T chart	I think that overall …
synthesise	What order do these work best in?	• Y chart	It could be … or it could mean … because …
evaluate/judge	How would you prioritise these?	• Venn diagram	In my opinion …
sequence	What does the data mean?	• balancing scales	The author is really saying …
rank	Why might this be the case?	• data chart	I agree/disagree because …
prioritise		• ranking	This seems to mean …
establish cause and effect		• PMI (Plus, Minus, Interesting)	Not everyone would agree …
infer		• SWOT (Strengths, Weaknesses, Opportunities, Threats)	This should go first because …
interpret		• KWFL (K is what pupils already Know, W is what they Want to know, F is where they can Find this out, and L is what they have already Learnt)	When you weigh up all the …
consider different viewpoints		• cycle circle	
reason		• twister	
		• flow chart	
		• continuum	
		• consequence or futures wheel	

predict and hypothesise. Pupils who have a right-brain thinking preference feel more confident with creative thinking situations in which they can generate new ideas and find, explore and consider options and alternatives.

Each of us uses both sides of our brain, but we often have a preferred – almost automatic – way of thinking, unless we are challenged. Using a range of thinking skills and strategies can extend pupils beyond their comfort zone. Working in non-preferred ways and with others with different thinking preferences and dispositions can be very powerful learning contexts. Such situations are likely to challenge pupils' thinking and engage them more fully in learning.

Organising learning to extend thinking requires teachers to have a sound knowledge of pupil abilities, skills, learning preferences, interests and needs. In addition, understanding types of thinking skills and knowing strategies to enhance these skills can create more thoughtful curricula (see page 6).

Thinking dispositions

A disposition is a person's tendency to use their abilities in particular ways. The tendencies are displayed frequently over time. Effective thinkers often display tendencies to be curious, critical, explorative and inquiring and to question, reason, clarify, organise and reflect on ideas and their own thinking. They are open-minded and creative in their thinking.

Thinking dispositions have been described by theorists in many different ways. The table on page 9 synthesises some of the commonly identified dispositions. The questions in the table can be used to prompt different thinking dispositions. They can be easily adapted for many areas of the curriculum: for example, for discussing texts, science experiments and social dilemmas.

When we plan for an excursion we need to think about it in different ways; for example:

Empathically:	What if some kids can't go? Should it be compulsory?
Open-mindedly:	I didn't think we'd get a say in the excursion.
Reflectively:	It's going to be scary to ring the excursion places.
Precisely:	We can't go overseas. What's the furthest we can go? What is the limit to the budget?

Thinking dispositions

Be curious

What do you wonder about?
What problems or issues are raised?
What questions would you ask the author/producer/designer/inventor?

Be precise

What are you sure about?
What examples can you give to explain or justify your thoughts?
Are there any gaps in what you know?
What could you explain about this to others?
What are the facts?

Be open-minded

What are some different perspectives?
What is something you have never thought of before?
What was unexpected or surprising?
What would you say/do differently?

Be organised

How can you sequence your ideas or issues from start to end?
What do you need to do to find out more?
What do you need to do next?
How could you solve this problem?

Be reflective and metacognitive

How would you sum up your ideas?
How have your thinking and feelings changed?
Have you answered your questions or do you have new questions?
What do you know that you didn't know before?
How effective was your thinking?
What has influenced your thinking?
What kind of thinking might you need to do more of?
What do you believe?

Be empathic

How do others feel about this?
What are some other points of view?
Is there a way of seeing this differently?
How might this affect others?
Are your views shared? By whom?

3 The role of the teacher

As with all skills, the role of the teacher in improving pupils' thinking is central to success. Teachers who deftly use a range of strategies to bring thinking to life in their classrooms know the importance of:

- **Thinking aloud** – modelling higher levels of thinking to pupils and letting them in on how different kinds of thinking 'work' for different purposes. By modelling and explicating a range of thinking skills, strategies and questions, we demonstrate that we are also thinkers and learners and we show pupils how to think.

- **Celebrating great thinking** – making time to acknowledge the wonderful thinking pupils do. Teachers record and display pupils' thinking and show they value the different ways in which pupils think about a topic or issue.

- **Making the teaching of thinking explicit in the classroom** – pupils know, for example, that they are learning how to think more creatively because the teacher has shared this purpose with them.

- **Questioning pupils in ways that extend and promote thinking** – using a range of question types is fundamental to effective thinking (see page 12).

- **Planning and organising for thinking** – as part of the classroom program (see page 12).

- **Teaching pupils strategies for thinking** – the most effective teachers of thinking are those who not only build the pupils' repertoire of strategies but also help pupils understand when and how to use them. It is no value to pupils to know how to do a Venn diagram, for example, if they do not understand how this strategy might be used and why.

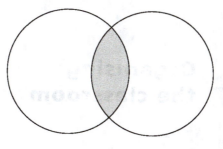

Venn diagrams are useful when comparing and contrasting.

The similar elements of two different things are shown in the central overlapping space.

4 Organising the classroom

This section outlines a range of ways to broaden and deepen thinking. We believe the guidelines and strategies are best used within the context of a learner-centred curriculum in which the content is significant and the learning tasks are purposeful. In other words, pupils need to be engaged in thinking about something worthwhile.

When organising for thinking, teachers can consider the way that they:

- question
- challenge
- encourage pupils to take risks
- arrange groups
- encourage engagement and participation.

Encourage questioning and create a thinking discourse

Thinking skills should become a topic for regular classroom discussion and reflection. Teachers should talk about the kind of thinking that is being used and is required. Pupils gradually learn to use 'the language of thinking' as they plan, discuss and reflect on their work. The role of the teacher in promoting classroom discourse and questioning about thinking is a significant one, but pupils need to do most of the thinking, questioning and talking in the classroom.

Effective questioning is at the core of effective thinking. In general, it is useful if teachers:

- **Plan challenging questions and be explicit about their purpose** – for example, different questions from the teacher will elicit different kinds of thinking from pupils:
  - What differences do you notice between these two websites? (Analytical)
  - What do you think the author wanted you to believe? (Critical)
  - How would you end the story? (Creative)
  - How did this article make you feel? (Reflective)
  - What are you noticing about your thinking? (Metacognitive)

- **Allow some 'think time' after questions and responses** – much research shows that when we provide pupils with more 'wait time' both after our questions and their responses, pupils are more likely to engage in the discussion and think more deeply about the topic.

- **Encourage pupils to reflect aloud** and to try to explain how and why they are thinking and feeling about certain issues.

- **Use pupil questions as a basis for thinking about, hypothesising, discussing, investigating and evaluating ideas** – the questions pupils devise often lead them to quality thinking and, when we use their questions, pupils are more likely to be engaged and interested in the ideas. The results of their investigations are worth reflecting on.

Why is junk food called 'junk'?

Are vegetarians healthier than meat eaters?

Why do people go on diets?

Do your tastebuds change as you get older?

How come the canteen sells lollies?

- Teach pupils how to ask different kinds of questions – the table on pages 14–15 shows a range of questions that both pupils and teachers can ask in order to activate different types of thinking. Teachers can model questions that they hope pupils will internalise and use at appropriate stages of the unit.

Early in the session/unit

Teacher questions	Pupil questions
What do you know about …?	What do I know about this topic/issue?
What can you already do?	What can I already do that would be useful?
What do you plan to do during this session? How do you plan to do this?	What plan can I make to achieve my task?
What do you remember/know/ understand from the last session	What do I remember/know/understand from last time?
What problems/questions do you have? What can you do about this?	What problems/questions do I have?
What do you think would be helpful to do/think about first?	What do I think would be a helpful starting point?

During the session/unit

Teacher questions	Pupil questions
What are you up to/doing? Why?	Where am I up to?
How will this help you?	How will this help me?
What do you need help with?	What do I need help with?
What do you plan to do next? Why?	What is my plan to move forward?
Do you know how to …?	How long will I need to do this? Do I need longer or can I get it done more quickly? How?
How long will you need to do this? Why?	
How can I help you?	Are the methods I am using effective?
What methods are you using?	What other ways could I do this?
Are these effective? What other methods could you use?	What have I learnt so far?
What have you learnt so far?	

After the session/unit

Teacher questions	Pupil questions
What have you learnt? Why? How?	What have I learnt? Why? How?
What can you now do that you couldn't do before?	What can I now do that I couldn't do before?
What do you now know that you didn't know before?	What do I know now that I didn't know before?
Now that you have done this today, what will you need to do next time?	Now that I have done this, what will I need to do next time?
What/who helped you to learn? How?	What/who helped me to learn? How?
What hindered your learning? Why?	What hindered my learning? Why?
What do you still need to do/learn?	What do I still need to do/learn?
Why do you think we did this?	What helped me do this?
	What was the purpose of this task?

Plan to challenge

Pupils will pay more attention to content and their own thinking and be more engaged if the content is challenging. Learning opportunities must allow for extension, creativity and critique of thinking. Open-ended tasks in which there are many possible paths and possibilities enable more pupils to be challenged but, as with all teaching strategies and approaches, they do not suit every learning purpose. For example, where prior knowledge needs to be determined – often at the beginning of tasks – closed questions may work best to quickly assess particular aspects of pupil thinking and knowledge. Also necessary are other approaches that allow the teacher to access pupil understandings and values that they may not have anticipated or planned for.

When we base our teaching on where pupils are currently at and where we think they can individually move to – as opposed to where we think they should be or hope they will be – we have real potential to help pupils move forward. Involving pupils in setting and negotiating their own goals can also increase the relevance for pupils. After all, they have the best idea of where they are and what they'd like to achieve.

Pupils' thinking can be challenged when we:

- ask questions that encourage higher-order thinking (for example, where pupils must analyse, synthesise, critique, create or apply).

- use significant generative questions as the basis for units of work; for example:

  - What makes a great friend?
  - What does it mean to be healthy?
  - What is art?
  - How do scientists work?
  - Why are invertebrates so important?

  There are no single closed answers to these questions. They require extended and complex thinking that develops over time.

- use open-ended activities that allow for a range of responses; for example, 'Design a new enclosure for our class pet'.

Risk-take to promote respect and reflection

In a classroom where risk-taking is encouraged, pupils are more likely to articulate their own thinking and respect others' opinions and rights. Honest, open and respectful communication requires constant attention and can be the subject of whole class reflection. Pupils learn much from the ways that teachers work with each other and talk to their pupils, and by the examples of talk and reflection that teachers highlight during discussions. Teachers can demonstrate the process of risk taking, showing that they value a range of opinions and reflect on the results of such discussions.

Cooperative group work to enhance thinking

While thinking is done in a person's head, changes to thinking are often a response to discussion with others or listening to other people's ideas. When cooperative group work is effective, many types of thinking might be enacted. For example, pupils might individually list some ideas about a topic. They bring these to the group and share their knowledge. As a group they could use various graphic organisers to compare and contrast ideas (see strategies on page 59). When the group has synthesised the information, they could create a solution or product that includes everyone's ideas. In addition, they might be asked to identify how their individual ideas have been broadened. This highlights the usefulness of collective expertise. Without shared talking, working and thinking time, various perspectives may not have been considered.

Cooperative learning also helps develop pupils' empathic thinking. In helping pupils to learn to work effectively with each other, we encourage them to think about how other pupils might be thinking and feeling within the group.

Philosophical discussions

One fruitful context for thinking together is a philosophical discussion. This is intended to engage pupils in higher-order thinking at concrete and abstract levels. Pupils are asked to explore issues and questions by discussing, justifying and evaluating reasons for ideas, beliefs and values. The teacher acts as a facilitator who may ask (and model) questions to clarify the direction of discussion and probe for and encourage depth of thinking, but they are only one voice in the classroom. They facilitate and guide rather than control and direct the discussion.

There are a range of excellent structures for developing what are often referred to as 'communities of inquiry' (Cam 1995; Golding 2002). The quality of philosophical discussions is enhanced when questioning is high level and based on two fundamental features: trust and inquiry. There are a number of protocols and structures for facilitating philosophical discussions, including 'Socratic questioning'.

In a Socratic question sequence, we select an issue for moral and ethical discussion and then work through questions in sequence. Sample statements for debate are:

Women are unfit to be prime minister.

Teachers get too many holidays.

The government should fund all schools equally.

1 **Source questions** – focus on the source of the information that led to the construction of the debatable statement.

2 **Support questions** – now think of additional information that might support the debatable statement.

3 **Conflicting views questions** – consider the views of people who would not support the debatable statement.

4 **Consequence questions** – what might be some social actions based on conclusions?

Pupils can then decide whether they accept or reject the debatable statement. (Based on Whitehead 2001)

Engaging more pupils in thinking

Even when we ask higher-order questions or when we select powerful content to activate thinking, the way we work with pupils can often result in only a minority of pupils being involved in the dialogue. Class discussions, in particular, are one forum in which teachers often try to encourage deeper thinking about a topic – but this can be the least effective way to have all pupils participate.

It is not just the quality of our questions but also the way we ask the questions that determines the degree to which pupils engage in thinking. The following simple techniques can make a big difference to participation in thoughtful discussion and learning.

■ As a general rule, keep whole class discussions short. Many pupils soon lose interest when they are gathered together as a big group that is 'directed' by the teacher.

■ When you do have whole class discussions, organise pupils in a circle so that everyone can see everyone else. This arrangement encourages pupils to have dialogue with each other – not just between individuals and the teacher.

■ Increase the number of small group discussions. Working with six pupils means that more pupils are likely to have a say and do some thinking.

■ Try some alternatives to 'hands up'. For example:

No hands up, please. I will give you some thinking time and then pick two people to share. What are some of the things we can do to protect this habitat?

OK. Thumbs up if you agree and thumbs down if you disagree with this statement – and be prepared to defend your answer.

Close your eyes everyone. Think about what we have discussed about what makes a group work well. I am going to give you 5 seconds to think. Be ready to share your answers with your group.

Jot down some of your creative ideas about how we could make this house. When you are ready, bring your jotters to the floor and I will ask you to share your best idea.

In these examples, the teacher is giving pupils thinking time and opportunities to 'rehearse' their thinking before they share with the group and to think with others before they decide about what to share. This creates greater accountability – anyone may be asked, not just the person who flings their hands up first.

- Using props such as talk or question 'tokens' (pupils have a number of tokens they can 'spend' during a discussion – see pages 61–62) or 'talking sticks' can focus pupils on really thinking about what they want to say rather than offering the first, often low-level thought that comes into their head.

- Finally, using probing questions and prompts can help pupils to think more deeply. Typically, we receive a response from a pupil and then move on to another question or another pupil. Take time to ask a pupil to expand their thinking – use prompts or clarifying phrases such as:

Tell me more about that idea …

Could you give us an example of what you mean?

Where did that idea come from?

What thinking did you do to come up with that?

Can you explain that in more detail?

Why is that idea important to you?

That's an interesting idea. Think a bit more about it and I will come back to you in a few minutes to hear more about it.

Maintaining eye contact and extending the engagement with individual pupils during discussions can really help pupils to think more deeply about their responses. The teacher's role is to guide them to more complex thinking.

When planning to develop thinking within the classroom program, the focus must be on the thinking type and/or skill required. This is determined by the needs of the pupils and the teaching and learning purposes, and relates to the intellectual challenge appropriate for the pupils in the class. While a variety of strategies is advantageous, the purpose must precede the choice of strategy. Pupils should be taught a range of strategies and why they are used, and should be able to identify and select them for themselves purposefully.

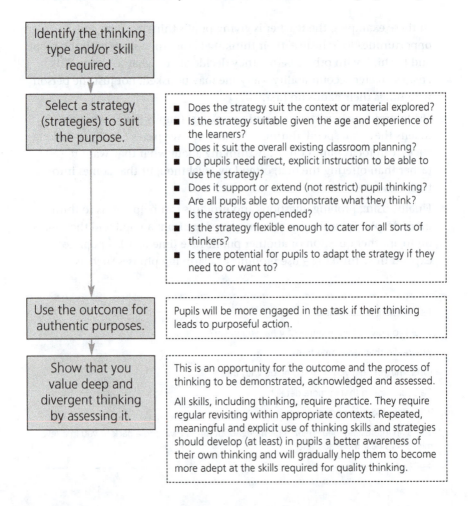

Identify the thinking type and/or skill required.

Select a strategy (strategies) to suit the purpose.

- Does the strategy suit the context or material explored?
- Is the strategy suitable given the age and experience of the learners?
- Does it suit the overall existing classroom planning?
- Do pupils need direct, explicit instruction to be able to use the strategy?
- Does it support or extend (not restrict) pupil thinking?
- Are all pupils able to demonstrate what they think?
- Is the strategy open-ended?
- Is the strategy flexible enough to cater for all sorts of thinkers?
- Is there potential for pupils to adapt the strategy if they need to or want to?

Use the outcome for authentic purposes.

Pupils will be more engaged in the task if their thinking leads to purposeful action.

Show that you value deep and divergent thinking by assessing it.

This is an opportunity for the outcome and the process of thinking to be demonstrated, acknowledged and assessed.

All skills, including thinking, require practice. They require regular revisiting within appropriate contexts. Repeated, meaningful and explicit use of thinking skills and strategies should develop (at least) in pupils a better awareness of their own thinking and will gradually help them to become more adept at the skills required for quality thinking.

Selecting strategies within a learning sequence

Teachers are becoming more familiar with various thinking tools such as de Bono's strategies, but these should not simply be taught in isolation. The tools should be used to develop appropriate thinking skills within the context of meaningful content. We need to teach thinking skills explicitly and also ensure that these skills are used in purposeful, contextualised ways. The table below shows an outline of a simple teaching sequence. Within the teaching sequence, we can use a variety of tools to develop skills in different types of thinking.

Stage in lesson or unit	Sample tasks or activities	Type of thinking
Beginning	Pupils identify prior knowledge, make predictions and pose questions.	Reflection and metacognition
	Sample strategies: *Think, pair, share* 1 Think about what you already know. 2 Join with a partner to discuss this. 3 Be prepared to share your ideas with the whole class. *Create a 'wonder wall' of questions.*	Creative thinking

What if ...?	What ...?	Would ...?
Where does ...?		How might ...?
Why ...?	How ...?	When ...?
Who ...?		Where ...?

| During | Information is gathered, critiqued and analysed.
Sample strategies:
View a video and make notes on a data chart.
Create a Venn diagram to compare information from two sources. | Logical and critical thinking |

Stage in lesson or unit	Sample tasks or activities	Type of thinking
End	Pupils reflect on their changing ideas, consider their knowledge in light of their prior knowledge and reflect on their own thinking. **Sample strategy:** *Use reflective sentence starters.*	Reflection and metacognition
	Pupils generate a range of solutions and consider the practical implications of each or innovate on an idea. **Sample strategy:** *Use de Bono's green hat thinking.* Use the green hat to think about some creative solutions to this problem. What is possible?	Creative and logical thinking
	Pupils carry out self-assessment and further goal setting. **Sample strategy:** *Return to the wonder wall.* Can we answer any of our questions? How did we find out?	Reflection

Strategies and activities

There are many frameworks for broadening and improving the range of thinking done in classrooms. In addition, a range of approaches and strategies that teachers and pupils can use offer ways to integrate thinking into the classroom program for meaningful purposes in enjoyable ways.

Each strategy may have several purposes, depending on how it is used and in what context, but the primary purpose is indicated to assist selection.

Thinking about feeling

Purpose or thinking type: Empathic and reflective

Using the *Thinking about Feeling* worksheet on page 58, pupils create labels to describe the feelings expressed by each character. The worksheet may be laminated and then cut into cards to be used for a variety of activities, such as:

- helping pupils to identify their feelings about a particular task or event
- matching cards to various characters in a story
- identifying how others in a cooperative group might be feeling.

Question in role

Purpose or thinking type: Empathic and creative

This strategy assists pupils to think about what is often inferred rather than made explicit in texts. Select a text to read to your pupils – or have them read it to themselves. The best texts are those that involve several characters, some of whom are in the background. The text may be a novel, film, picture storybook or a non-fiction account of an event such as a newspaper report.

1 Once the text has been read, organise pupils into small groups.

2 Select a background character from the story about whom little is said by the author.

3 One pupil in the group represents this character.

4 Other pupils in the group prepare and then ask the character questions about their feelings and involvement in the story.

5 They may question the character as if they are 'newspaper reporters' to enhance the fun of the session.

Here, there, everywhere

Purpose or thinking type: Critical and creative

This strategy helps pupils to analyse a text by making links between it and other texts and issues. The strategy is simple yet very effective. The text can be fiction or non-fiction and can be a film, song, novel, picture storybook, news report or still image. This strategy often works best when the text relates to a topic being studied by the pupils as it is easier for them to make connections and draw on prior knowledge.

Read or have the pupils read the text. Now ask the pupils to write down or share with others their responses to the following questions:

1 **Here:** What is something in your life right now that this text reminds you of? How does this relate to you?

2 **There:** What is something in another text or someone else's life that this text reminds you of?

3 **Everywhere:** What other issues or ideas in the world does this text relate to? What other connections can you make?

Pupils may use a simple visual organiser such as a concept map to demonstrate the connections they are making.

Marvellous metaphors

Purpose or thinking type: Creative

Metaphors and analogies can be a great method to assist pupils to explore ideas in depth and also to give teachers an opportunity to assess pupil understanding of a topic. Metaphors work best when the pupil has some background in the topic – often towards the end of a unit of work. There are many ways to challenge pupils to explore metaphors. Try the following.

- Give pupils an analogy and have them brainstorm their responses; for example: 'Planet Earth is like the human body.'
- As pupils become more familiar with the technique, have them select their own metaphors or analogies on a topic.
- Using actual objects can also be a stimulating way to think about metaphors. Give pupils a variety of objects. Ask them to choose one of the objects as a metaphor for the topic and be ready to explain to others why they have chosen it.

Concept attainment

Purpose or thinking type: Logical or critical

This strategy encourages pupils to think for themselves. Present pupils with a 'data set' of items, pictures or words that have criteria in common; for example, a set of invertebrates that live in water.

Pupils then try to add to the data set without being told what the criteria are. If they select an item that belongs, welcome them to the 'club'; if the item does not fit the criteria, it is put aside and the pupil is encouraged to keep trying. As the data set is added to, pupils gradually work out what all the items have in common and the criteria can be revealed.

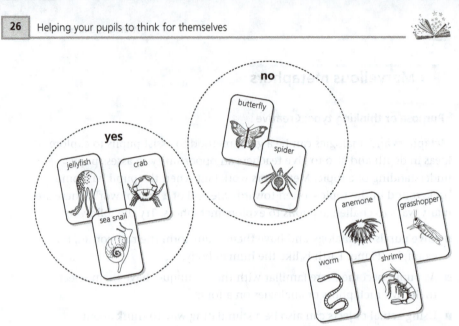

SCAMPER

Purpose or thinking type: Creative

Using the SCAMPER (Substitute, Combine, Adapt, Modify/Magnify/Minimise, Put to another use, Eliminate and Remove/Reverse) framework, creative questions and thinking can be developed by the teacher or pupils. While some contexts might use all seven facets of SCAMPER, it is better – and easier – to select those that suit your purposes. This technique can be applied to text analysis or other aspects of a unit of work. The following questions are an example of how to think differently about school camps.

S	**Substitute** (a person or object)	If you were to change one activity what would you replace it with?
C	**Combine** (blend and bring together materials, ideas or situations)	Think about two camps you have already been on. Can you combine the best parts of each camp to come up with ideas for a really great camp?
A	**Adapt** (adjust to new purposes or conditions)	How would you change the camp if your parents were coming along for the week?
M	**Modify/magnify/minimise** (enlarge, reduce or change size, quality, frequency)	What would you like to do more often at camp?
P	**Put to another use** (for another purpose, situation or way of doing things)	Imagine we had to stay at the campsite for several months and we had to continue your schooling there. What would need to happen if camp became school?
E	**Eliminate** (take away or leave out a part or whole element)	If you were to eliminate a problem of the camp, what would it be? What would you want to keep?
R	**Remove/reverse** (change sequence or layout)	What might have happened if there were no pupil camp duties?

BAR

Purpose or thinking type: Creative

First developed by Tony Ryan (1990) this is a similar but simpler version of SCAMPER, as it also requires creative thinking by pupils. This works well for content for which designing is involved such as technology and science topics. For example, pupils might be asked to consider the existing design (or their own design) of an object (or scenario) and change it using BAR (Bigger, Add, Remove/Reduce/Replace).

	Facet of BAR	Example: started as a drink bottle – ended up as a scoop
B	**Bigger** (make a part or the whole bigger)	made the opening bigger
A	**Add** (add something to make it more appealing, practical or adaptable, etc)	added a handle
R	**Remove, reduce or replace** (take away a part, make a part smaller or replace a part)	removed the bottom

Cause and effect wheels

Purpose or thinking type: Logical/critical and creative

Cause and effect wheels (also called consequence or futures wheels) are a great way to help pupils think laterally about a topic and to consider the implications of the issues arising from it. This is a useful way of reinforcing the concept of cause and effect, and can also be used as a decision-making tool.

Cause and effect wheels begin with a cause or a 'what if', which is written in the centre of the page. For example:

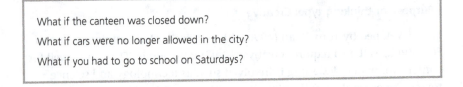

What if the canteen was closed down?

What if cars were no longer allowed in the city?

What if you had to go to school on Saturdays?

Pupils then create a cause and effect wheel showing as many of the consequences they can think of. Each consequence generates further consequences – represented by adding a new linking line.

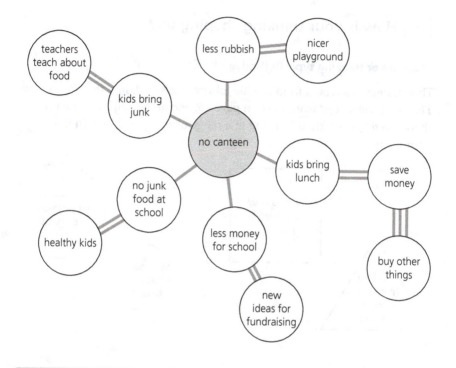

6–3–1

Purpose or thinking type: Reflective, logical and critical

This is an excellent strategy for helping pupils to synthesise their understanding of a topic.

1 Begin by asking pupils to brainstorm a list of six words they think are most important and relevant to the topic.

2 Ask pupils to get together with a partner, share their lists and come up with an agreed common list of the three most important words.

3 Each pair then shares their list of three with another pair and must agree on the most important word, which can come from their lists or can be a new one they all agree on.

4 Each group shares their word with the whole class. Pupils should be encouraged to reflect on the main words that have been chosen and why.

How is your thinking shaping up?

Purpose or thinking type: Reflective

This strategy is adapted from Neville Johnson (2003). Using the *How Is Your Thinking Shaping Up?* worksheet on page 56, encourage pupils to use the shapes to reflect on their learning in a range of ways, as shown in the example below.

Behind the scene

Purpose or thinking type: Critical

This strategy requires pupils to focus on an image such as a photo, painting or other visual text. The following questions are used to guide thinking. Each question can be written on the face of a foam dice and tossed by the group. The question that lands 'face up' is then brainstormed by the group and their ideas shared.

- What is going on in the picture?
- Who might have created this image and why?
- What did the creator of this image want the viewer to feel and know?

- What is not shown in this image? What is excluded?

- How has the creator of the image positioned us as viewers? What angle are we looking from? Where does the image draw your eyes and why?

- If you could ask the creator of this image one question, what would it be?

Know, feel, wonder, do

Purpose or thinking type: Reflective

This strategy is a good way to encourage pupils to think more deeply about artworks (visual, performing or musical).

Using the *Know, Feel, Wonder, Do* worksheet on page 57, pupils respond to each question. Once they have completed the reflection, they share their response with each other and discuss how their responses compared.

Moral dilemmas

Purpose or thinking type: Critical

Organise pupils into groups of three. Each person in the group must take on one of the following roles:

- decision maker

- negative voice

- positive voice.

Explain to pupils that you will present them with a dilemma – a scenario that requires a decision to be made involving several competing factors. The decision maker must decide what to do. The pupils representing the positive and negative voices sit either side of the decision maker and take it in turns to argue 'for' and 'against'. After several minutes of play, the decision maker weighs up the arguments and presents their final decision. Once pupils have practised the technique, they can create their own moral dilemmas to present to others.

Sample dilemma

Your best friend has invited you out for her birthday. You are the only one who has been invited to be part of the special day. You are thrilled and you are about to say 'yes' when you remember that you promised to go to your little brother's first football final. He is very excited about you being there and has told the whole team that his big sister is coming especially to cheer them on. He has been talking about the match for weeks – but it is on at exactly the same time as the party. Should you go to the birthday or not?

Rebranding

Purpose or thinking type: Creative, critical and reflective

'Rebranding' (Whitehead 2001) challenges pupils to think about an idea or object in many different ways. It can help reveal the depth of a pupil's understanding of a specific topic. It is a technique used by advertisers to persuade an audience to change their perception of a product.

To begin the process, ask pupils to complete a statement related to the topic or issue under discussion: 'It's not just [a] … it is also [a] …'

For example: It's not just alcohol …
it is also an addictive substance.
it is also a source of misery.
it is also the cause of many car accidents.
it is also a way to help people relax.
it is also a drink served at many celebrations.

Discuss how this rebranding has helped or changed pupils' thinking.

Three-step definitions

Purpose or thinking type: Logical and reflective

This excellent strategy, adapted from Hamston and Murdoch (2004), can be used before reading or viewing a text or to find out about what pupils know at the beginning of a unit of work.

Pupils draw up a four-column chart or table. In the first column, they list important words that appear in the text. In the remaining columns, they write their own definition, a dictionary definition and then how they think the word might be used in the text. Hypothesising and thinking ahead of reading or viewing helps engage pupils with the text and enhances comprehension.

Word	What I think it means	What the dictionary says it means	How it might be used in this text

Choice projects (based on thinking)

Purpose or thinking type: All

Choice projects offer pupils a range of tasks to direct thinking about a topic in a particular way. These can be used as independent learning contracts. To design these, teachers first identify the thinking they want pupils to do, and then develop activities to activate this sort of thinking. A sample is included below.

Clean up your act

Compare	Evaluate	Analyse
Use a Venn diagram to compare two different types of household products.	Choose a cleaning product and an environmentally friendly alternative. List criteria to evaluate their effectiveness (include cost).	Find out why people choose certain products. What are the main influencing factors?

Perspectives	Reflect	Imagine
Choose a cleaning product. What are three different perspectives about its effect on the environment?	Think carefully about your use of products. Which ones could you do without? Why? Think of possible substitutes.	You are a product marketer. How would you market a new product to appeal to a range of buyers?

Classify	Justify	Invent
Make a list of 20 household products. Put them into groups and label each.	The government has decided to decrease the number of available household cleaning products. Which would you recommend be discontinued? Why?	Create an environmentally friendly cleaning product.

Reflection bookmarks

Purpose or thinking type: Critical and reflective

Reflection bookmarks (see *Reflection Bookmarks* on page 53 and *Mark My Words Bookmarks* worksheets on pages 54–55) have been designed to cue pupils to do particular types of thinking as they read or view texts, but could be used for other more general thinking contexts. There are four bookmarks in the worksheets: one specifically for reading and viewing, a generic one and two with open-ended statements ('I noticed …' and 'I wonder …') on which pupils could record their observations and questions as they work.

Stepping stones reflection

Purpose or thinking type: Reflective

Prepared sentence strips (see *Stepping Stones* worksheet on page 52) can be used to stimulate individual, small group tasks or whole group reflective discussions. See the examples below.

- I am wondering about …
- My question is ….
- I feel …
- I think we should …
- I'm not sure about …
- I think we're learning about this because …
- I have learnt …
- The most important thing that I have learnt is …
- Now I plan to …
- I can now …
- I now know …
- I will always remember …
- I still wonder …
- I will evaluate my …
- This is important to me because …
- I was surprised that …
- I am proud of …
- I wish I had …
- I need to improve …
- The best part of this is …
- I got a lot better at …

I NOW KNOW…

I WISH …

I CAN NOW…

Using graphic organisers

Purpose or thinking type: All

Graphic organisers (see *Making Thinking Visual with Graphic Organisers* worksheet on page 59), also called visual organisers, can be a powerful way to develop thinking skills and, in particular, to make pupils' thinking more explicit both to themselves and to others. Graphic organisers are widely used beyond the classroom. They can be a highly effective form of communication that requires few words. Teachers can adapt organisers to suit a range of purposes, but it is important that the intended purpose is clear and the chosen organiser is the most suitable for the kind of thinking involved. It is a good idea to build a classroom display showing the different kinds of organisers that are available.

Frequently asked questions (and trouble-shooting)

How can thinking be assessed?

If thinking is valued as a key curriculum objective, we must take time to assess pupils' development. Pupils know the most about their own thinking; therefore we should involve them in assessment. However, like teachers, pupils must have an understanding of the type of thinking they are assessing and a language to describe it. Linking goal setting to reflection and self-assessment is a worthwhile process for pupils of all ages.

No single assessment strategy can suit all learners or show what they know; therefore a variety of strategies has better potential to help pupils clarify and demonstrate what and how they think. Journals and graphic organisers, for example, have been used successfully for these purposes, but many other techniques can be equally useful, depending on the purpose of the task and assessment. Many of the activities suggested in this book provide teachers and pupils with evidence of their thinking skills. It is important for teachers to clarify what kind of thinking they are looking and listening for when planning their programs, as this will help sharpen their capacity to assess thinking.

What about those pupils who don't seem to want to think deeply?

As with all learning skills, pupils will be more motivated when they are interested in what they are thinking about or see a real purpose for their thinking. You only have to watch the way pupils can apply sophisticated and complex thinking to electronic games to know that deep thinking is possible – the context and purpose may make a difference! When the thinking strategies we have outlined in this book are applied in context – and when the context is purposeful, relevant and engaging – more pupils will be prepared to meet the challenge of deeper thinking.

Importantly, deep thinking needs to be celebrated in the classroom. Teachers can make the world of difference by showing how much they value the efforts made by pupils to persist with their thinking and to take their thinking beyond the surface. Involve pupils in thinking deeply about things they are interested in – we have heard some wonderfully deep conversations about topics such as football, the world of fashion and responsible pet ownership. Focusing on topics of interest to children will help build their confidence to apply strategies and techniques to topics and problems beyond their experience.

Isn't it too much to expect young pupils to perform higher-order thinking?

Even in the early years of schooling, pupils are capable of identifying what they think, how they and others think, and how their thinking can be extended and improved. We know that even before they come to school, young children ask questions and make observations that illustrate their capacity to think about their world in creative and reflective ways. One of the most important ways we can assist young pupils is to help them make their thinking 'visible' – this can be done by scribing and displaying their questions and ideas, introducing them to simple visual organisers or taping discussions and playing them back to them, focusing on how they are thinking. When working with young pupils, it is particularly important to locate this teaching within the context of pupils' everyday experiences. For example, an argument in the playground can be sorted out using de Bono's hats ('We need to put on our red hat to think about how we are feeling …') and responses to picture storybooks can be deliberately geared around thinking strategies ('Let's try and be empathic thinkers – what do you think the ugly sisters would be thinking right now?'). Using the language of thinking with young children soon gives them the confidence to talk about what is 'going on in their heads'. The earlier we start this, the better.

What content is rich and meaningful enough to develop thinking?

Of course, pupils can think about anything and everything – but there is no doubt that the content we ask them to think about can make a difference to the level of thinking that is encouraged in the classroom. Some topics lend themselves more to higher-order thinking than others – although it is ultimately the questions we ask and the challenges we provide that make the most difference. In thinking-oriented classrooms, teachers are conscious of the need to explore topics that are complex and go way beyond fact-finding. One of the most effective vehicles for teaching thinking is to use inquiry-based units of work as part of the classroom programming. Such units of work explore, over an extended period of time, robust concepts and significant questions about the way the world works and actively involve pupils in questioning, thinking, seeking information and drawing their own conclusions.

We have found that when topics link easily to rich concepts, there are better opportunities for pupils to use higher-level thinking (see page 40 for some examples of such concepts). The topics we select for inquiry should lend themselves to the exploration of these concepts.

Sample concepts and topics

If we want pupils to think more deeply about...	Then we might plan an inquiry into...
change, time, cycles	how popular culture has changed over generations and the influences on this
diversity, identity, belonging	how and why people migrate to a new country and how this experience affects their identity
systems, interdependence, cause and effect	how materials can be used to create a variety of constructions and what is involved in the building process

Rich concepts for deep thinking

- adaptation
- behaviour
- cause and effect
- change
- changing lifestyles
- citizenship
- communication
- community
- conflict and cooperation
- conservation
- consumption
- culture
- customs and rituals
- cycles
- development
- distribution
- diversity
- ecological sustainability
- energy
- environment
- gender equity
- human rights
- Indigenous people
- institutions
- interaction
- interdependence
- invention and design
- work and leisure

- justice, rights and responsibilities
- life and living
- living and non-living
- location
- mobility
- needs and wants
- organisation
- patterns
- personal safety
- place and space
- power and control
- production
- relationships
- resources
- revolution
- rites of passage
- ritual
- roles, rules and laws
- social justice
- society and socialisation
- spirituality
- supply and demand
- survival
- systems
- the physical world
- tradition
- transitions
- wellbeing

(Adapted from Murdoch & Hornsby 1998)

How can thinking be incorporated into an already crowded curriculum?

The best way to improve pupils' thinking skills is to embed the skills into a challenging curriculum rather than see it as a separate part of the program. However, there is no doubt that we need time to make the teaching of thinking explicit to pupils – to 'press the pause button' and reflect and talk about the thinking we are doing. Many teachers we have worked with have deliberately planned to spend more time using fewer activities to encourage pupils to think more deeply. Similarly, teachers are also now reducing the number of units of study they might cover in a year to enable the time and space needed to 'go deeper' into particular concepts. Making time to think means examining our priorities – it is not so much about needing more time, rather changing the way we use time. We need to ask ourselves how the pupils' time is being spent. For example, spending time to make visual organisers look good makes no difference to the thinking and learning the pupil is doing. By clarifying the purposes of the activities we provide for pupils, we can decide which elements of tasks to give most time. In short, we should be spending more time on the things that make the most impact on pupil thinking and learning.

7 Tips for the teacher

The following tips summarise key points that underpin effective teaching for thinking in the classroom.

- When you are planning, think about the thinking skills you want to focus on.
- Show that you value thinking by making time for reflection.
- Use a variety of questions and be explicit about the purposes.
- Involve pupils in posing questions and self-questioning.
- Ensure that the level of intellectual challenge is appropriate for all pupils.
- Use pupils' own goals for self-assessment purposes.
- Include a variety of thinking types and strategies in the program.
- Be a risk taker and encourage pupils to take risks and reflect on the results.
- Use pupil investigation results to plan authentic action.
- Ensure that assessment recognises thinking (process and product).
- Incorporate cooperative learning strategies into the classroom.
- To provide a balance, keep track of the thinking skills and strategies you have used.

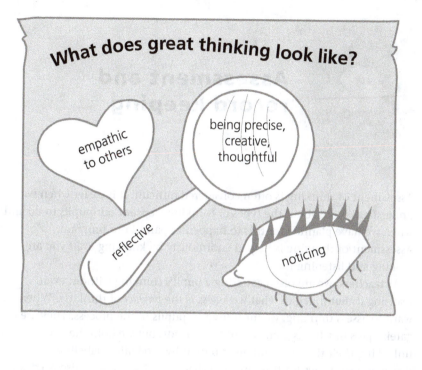

What does great thinking look like?

empathic to others

being precise, creative, thoughtful

reflective

noticing

8 Assessment and record keeping

Assessment of thinking is often considered difficult. It is easier when we understand more about the types of thinking we want our pupils to do and when we have planned for this to happen as part of our program. Assessment of thinking is helped enormously by knowing *what* you are looking and listening for.

As teachers, we are often assessing a pupil's thinking without even realising it. But much of what we assess is the *product* of thinking. When we want to assess thinking, we must involve pupils in the process. They are the gatekeepers of what is going on in their heads, but we hold the key to unlocking their thinking and describing it by modelling, labelling and discussing strategies for thinking and their effectiveness – as discussed earlier in this book.

Assessment of thinking is, therefore, made more possible when we:

■ know what it is we are looking and listening for

■ use strategies that help pupils make their thinking more 'visible and audible'

■ involve pupils in the process.

Involve pupils in assessment and goal setting

If we want to promote pupil thinking, involving pupils in the assessment process and personal goal setting is important. If goal setting is part of a program, time must be allowed for regular reflection on progress towards goals. This reflection will be the context for further self-assessment and could lead to modifying goals, further assessment and so on. The following examples are ways to include pupils in the assessment process.

- Ask pupils to identify their own thinking preferences and discuss ways to enhance thinking with the whole brain.

> When I am working in a group I usually think: What do other people think? What do other people feel? I usually feel a bit unsure of myself but I could be a bit more like a detective and ask: What do I know for certain? And not let my doubts get in the way. I could be more like an explorer and think: What is possible?

- Use pupil reflections on their own thinking as a basis for negotiating ways of working. For example, pupils may identify that they mostly use logical thinking when approaching tasks. The teacher might then ask them to use a creative-thinking strategy when presenting their ideas.
- Create class charts of useful questions for self- and peer-assessment purposes.

Thinking for yourself

Have you thought about . . .

- What needs to be done?
- What you already know?
- A plan of action?
- If you have any questions that need answering?
- What strategies would be useful?
- What resources might be needed?
- If there is another way to do it?
- What checking needs to be done?

- Involve pupils in program evaluation. Ask them for their critical feedback on the value of a particular lesson, unit or course. This has a different purpose to self-assessment. It involves pupils thinking through learning purposes and outcomes, and shows pupils that teachers value their ideas.

Using reflection – journals

Reflective journals or 'thinking books' are an effective vehicle for ongoing assessment of pupils' thinking skills. There are many different kinds of journals and they serve a range of purposes. For example, teachers might ask pupils to keep a journal to:

- reflect on how they are feeling about their work
- record their progress during an inquiry
- evaluate goals they have achieved
- communicate with the teacher in written form
- keep a private record of their feelings
- identify the learning that comes from an activity sequence
- collect thoughts and ideas that can be used later for writing, artwork or other tasks.

In the early years, pupils can participate in creating a whole class journal to collectively record and reflect on learning. A whole class journal can be an excellent way to model reflective thinking, as the teacher thinks aloud and writes in front of or with the class. Journals may also be kept by a group to record their progress through a cooperative activity.

Individual journals can take many forms. Here are some suggestions.

- **Open-ended, unstructured journals** – pupils simply draw or write about their learning.

---

8 March

Today we worked for the second time on the fundraising task. We got some information but Rhys put it away before I could read it. Hopefully he can find it next time. I have to mention it to him but I don't want him to go off! It's hard to work with a partner if they keep losing the information but then again it would be hard if we had to work it out by ourselves. I think this project is pretty useless unless we really do it. I'd like to do it but we'd need more time to plan it because we don't want to lose all our money if no one buys our raffle tickets.

■ **Double or triple entry journals** – pupils record their thinking using a staged sequence such as the following:

What I did	Why I did it	What I learnt
Today I interviewed my grandma about her life when she was my age.	I am gathering information from people of different age groups to find out about how childhood is changing over time. I am also practising my interviewing skills.	My grandma's life was very different to mine. She had to do lots more jobs around the house. She didn't even have TV! I need to work on note taking.

■ **Dialogue journals** – dialogue journals are generally written between the pupil and teacher, but can also be kept between pupils. In these journals, pupils record their thinking and feeling and the teacher responds in writing. Teacher responses can be a useful way to prompt deeper thinking, as the example below shows.

> I didn't get my maths work finished today because everyone at my table was talking too much.
> Erin
>
> It must be frustrating to still have more work to do, Erin. You made a good start though! What will you do next time? How could you solve your problem?
> Ms Jones
>
> Maybe I need to sit somewhere else in maths time.
> Erin

Journal writing is *one* vehicle that effectively supports reflective thinking. Like all strategies, however, it can be overused and those pupils who like to show their thinking in other ways – such as talking, artwork and drama – can tire of the task. To ensure that journal writing continues to be an engaging thinking task, make sure you:

■ vary the kind of journals you use

- model the language expected
- avoid 'doing' journals for everything
- encourage pupils to share journals with each other to find out other ways of approaching the task
- make the time needed for worthwhile reflections
- focus on the thinking, not the spelling or handwriting – direct the main feedback to the purpose of the task.

The *Thinking Checklist* below can be used to help pupils assess their own thinking, as shown in their journals.

Thinking Checklist for Pupils

Ways of thinking	Questions and starters	Date I did this	Example of when I did this	Evidence (tick)
Reflectively and metacognitively				
Ask self questions Question Remember ideas Make decisions Use ideas another time Go back and check Think about others' views	I wonder if … I need to know … I now can … I have changed my thinking/feelings. Next time I will … I can use that idea. What's another viewpoint?			
Creatively				
Challenge ideas Adapt ideas Imagine Invent	What if I …? Suppose you …? If I added … There must be other ways. I think … will happen if we … Why can't we try a new way? What are other possibilities?			

Thinking Checklist for Pupils (continued)

Ways of thinking	Questions and starters	Date I did this	Example of when I did this	Evidence (tick)
Logically and critically				
Organise (ideas, work) Find relevant parts or information Prioritise Predict Synthesise (draw ideas together) Examine Evaluate or judge Reason	Put together this means … How could I organise my ideas? When you weigh up all the … If you do … then … I think that overall … It could be … or it could mean … because … In my opinion … I agree/disagree because … The most important part …			

Overall comments

(Adapted from Murdoch & Wilson 2004)

Proformas for the classroom

9

Stepping Stones

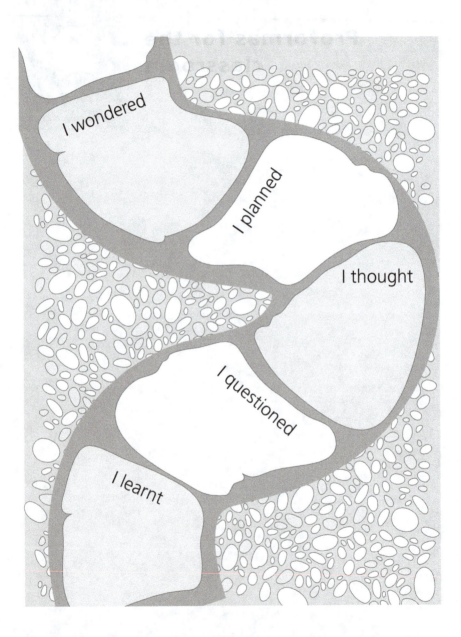

Reflection Bookmarks

Think about it

- How you felt and why

- What surprised you

- What changes you have noticed

- How the ideas could be related to your life

- Interesting, puzzling or new words

- What this reminds you of

- A motto that could be extracted from the ideas

- How this is similar or different to other ideas on the same topic

- What the big ideas are

Think about it

As you read, note:

- The big and recurrent issues

- The author's intentions

- How you felt and why

- Things that are funny, surprising, scary, etc

- Quotable quotes

- Interesting, puzzling or new words

- A sentence that you like

- The author's meaning

Mark My Words Bookmarks

Mark my words

I noticed . . .

....
....
....
....
....
....
....
....
....
....
....

Mark my words

I wonder . . .

....
....
....
....
....
....
....
....
....
....
....

Mark My Words Bookmarks (cont.)

Mark my words

I feel...

....

....

....

....

....

....

....

....

....

....

....

Mark my words

I know...

....

....

....

....

....

....

....

....

....

....

....

How Is Your Thinking Shaping Up?

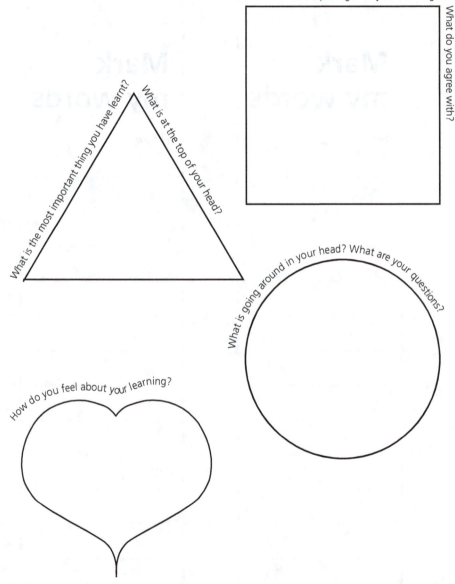

What is squaring with your thinking?

What do you agree with?

What is the most important thing you have learnt?

What is at the top of your head?

What is going around in your head? What are your questions?

How do you feel about your learning?

Know, Feel, Wonder, Do

KNOW

What did you learn from this? What new ideas or information did this give you?

FEEL

How do you feel about this? Draw or describe your feelings.

WONDER

What does this make you wonder? Write your questions.

DO

How might this change the way you create your next work? What could you do that uses some of the ideas or techniques you have seen or heard?

Name of artwork: _____

Thinking about Feeling

Create labels to describe the feeling shown in each illustration.

Making Thinking Visual with Graphic Organisers

Sample graphic organisers

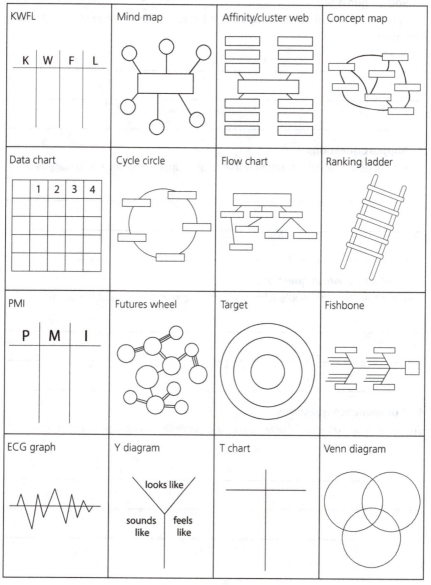

KWFL	Mind map	Affinity/cluster web	Concept map
Data chart	Cycle circle	Flow chart	Ranking ladder
PMI	Futures wheel	Target	Fishbone
ECG graph	Y diagram	T chart	Venn diagram

KWFL: K W F L

Data chart: 1 2 3 4

PMI: P M I

Y diagram: looks like / sounds like / feels like

Socratic Questions

Use the questions below to discuss issues and questions.

1 Source questions

Focus on the source of the information that led to the construction of the debatable statement.

_____

_____

_____

2 Support questions

Now think of additional information that might support the debatable statement.

_____

_____

_____

3 Conflicting views questions

Consider the views of people who would not support the debatable statement.

_____

_____

_____

4 Consequence questions

What might be some social actions based on conclusions (accept or reject the debatable statement)?

_____

_____

_____

Talk Tokens

Talk **token**	Talk **token**	Talk **token**	Talk **token**
Talk **token**	Talk **token**	Talk **token**	Talk **token**
Talk **token**	Talk **token**	Talk **token**	Talk **token**
Talk **token**	Talk **token**	Talk **token**	Talk **token**
Talk **token**	Talk **token**	Talk **token**	Talk **token**
Talk **token**	Talk **token**	Talk **token**	Talk **token**

Question Tokens

Question **token**	Question **token**	Question **token**	Question **token**
Question **token**	Question **token**	Question **token**	Question **token**
Question **token**	Question **token**	Question **token**	Question **token**
Question **token**	Question **token**	Question **token**	Question **token**
Question **token**	Question **token**	Question **token**	Question **token**
Question **token**	Question **token**	Question **token**	Question **token**

Thinking Audit

REFLECTIVE THINKING AND METACOGNITION

Have you asked your pupils to:

- recall what they know, feel, believe and have experienced?
- summarise their learning so far?
- plan for their own learning?
- ask questions about their own thinking, learning and the world?
- pose questions about what they know or have learnt or want to learn?
- be involved in their own action planning?
- decide about the learning process?
- apply their ideas to another situation or their life?
- judge their own progress?
- review what and how they have learnt?
- consider how their ideas have changed?
- consider how others might feel or think about the issue?

CREATIVE THINKING

Have you asked your pupils to:

- create original ideas?
- adapt ideas by adding, expanding or changing ideas?
- find and consider alternatives or solutions?
- challenge assumptions?
- imagine how things could be?
- make predictions or hypothesise about what they might find out?

LOGICAL AND CRITICAL THINKING

Have you asked your pupils to:

- organise and classify information and ideas?
- examine and critique data and information?
- hypothesise about ideas?
- judge or evaluate ideas?
- rank and prioritise ideas?
- interpret and make inferences about data?
- analyse data and information?
- generalise about ideas and findings?
- synthesise collected data or diverse data sets?
- sequence ideas and plans?
- deduce cause and effect relationships?

Further reading

Abbot, C. and Wilks, S. (2000) *I Think ...*, Australian Children's Television Foundation, Fitzroy.

Baird, J. (1998) 'A view of quality in teaching' in B.J. Fraser and K. Tobin (eds), *International Handbook of Science Education*, Dordrecht, Netherlands, pp. 153–67.

Cam, P. (1995) *Thinking Together*, PETA, Marrickville.

Costa, A. (1992) *The School as a Home for the Mind*, Hawker Brownlow Education, Melbourne.

Dalton, J. (1985) *Adventures in Thinking*, Nelson, South Melbourne.

Dewey, J. (1933) *How We Think: A Restatement of the Relation of Reflective Thinking to the Educative Process* (revised edn), Heath, Boston.

Eberle, B. (1990) *Scamper on: For Creative Imagination Development*, Hawker Brownlow Education, Melbourne.

Frangheim, E. (1998) *Reflections on Classroom Thinking Strategies*, Rodin Educational, Loganholme.

Golding, C. (2002) *Connecting Concepts: Thinking Activities for Students*, ACER, Camberwell.

Hamston, J. and Murdoch, K. (2004) *Australia Kaleidoscope*, Curriculum Corporation and AEF, Carlton South.

Jensen, E. (1998) *Super Teaching*, Focus Education, South Australia.

Johnson, N. (2003) Unpublished presentation, Melbourne.

Ministry of Education (1989) *Learning to Learn: Investigating Effective Learning Strategies*, Melbourne.

Murdoch, K. and Hornsby, D. (1998) *Planning Curriculum Connections*, Eleanor Curtain, Armadale.

Murdoch, K. and Wilson, J. (2004) *Learning Links*, Curriculum Corporation, Carlton South.

O'Brien, K. and White, D. (2001) *The Thinking Platform*, KD, NSW.

Pohl, M. (1997) *Teaching Thinking Skills in the Primary Years: A Whole School Approach*, Hawker Brownlow Education, Melbourne.

Pohl, M. (2000a) *Learning to Think, Thinking to Learn: Models and Strategies to Develop a Classroom Culture of Thinking*, Hawker Brownlow Education, Melbourne.

Pohl, M. (2000b) *Teaching Complex Thinking*, Hawker Brownlow Education, Melbourne.

Ryan, T. (1990) *Thinkers Keys*, self-published, Queensland.

Splitter, L. and Sharp, A. (1995) *Teaching for Better Thinking*, ACER, Camberwell.

Ward, C. (2001) *Teaching to Learn*, Accelerated Learning Institute, Christchurch, NZ.

Ward, C. and Daley, J. (1993) *Learning to Learn: Strategies for Accelerating Learning and Boosting Performance*, self-published, Christchurch, NZ.

Whitehead, D. (2001) *Top Tools for Literacy and Learning*, Pearson, NZ.

Wilks, S. (2004) (ed.) *Designing a Thinking Curriculum*, Australian Academy of the Arts, Melbourne.

Wilson, J. and Wing Jan, L. (1993) *Thinking for Themselves*, Eleanor Curtain, Armadale.

Wilson, J. and Wing Jan, L. (1993) *Self-assessment for Students*, Eleanor Curtain, Armadale.

Wilson, J. and Wing Jan, L. (2003) *Focus on Inquiry*, Curriculum Corporation, Carlton South.